piano • vocal • guitar

Dixie Chicks *fly*

ISBN 0-634-01263-0

HAL•LEONARD®
CORPORATION
7777 W. BLUEMOUND RD. P.O. BOX 13819 MILWAUKEE, WI 53213

Visit Hal Leonard Online at
www.halleonard.com

Dixie Chicks fly

contents

READY TO RUN

Words and Music by MARTIE SEIDEL
and MARCUS HUMMON

12

oh, _____ I'm read-y to run, _____ I'm read - y.

Repeat and Fade

N.C.

Optional Ending
G5

IF I FALL YOU'RE GOING DOWN WITH ME

Words and Music by ANNIE ROBOFF
and MATRACA BERG

Moderately

Was it the pull of the moon, now ba - by, that led you to my door? ___ You say the night's got you act - in' cra - zy, I think it's some-thin' more. ___

15

COWBOY TAKE ME AWAY

Words and Music by MARTIE SEIDEL
and MARCUS HUMMON

Original key: F# major. This edition has been transposed up one half-step to be more playable.

CODA

Clos - er to you.

Cow - boy, take me a - way, clos - er to you.

Instrumental ad lib.

COLD DAY IN JULY

Words and Music by
RICHARD LEIGH

The moon is full, ___ my arms are emp - ty.

All night ___ long I've plead - ed and cried. ___

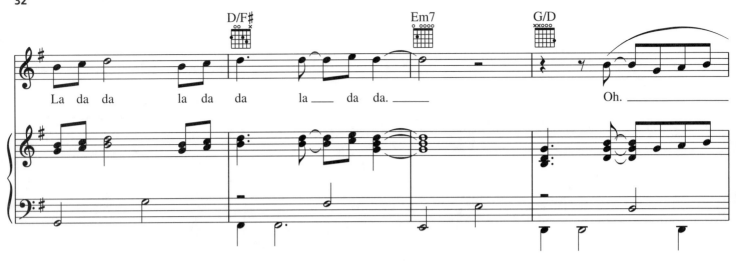

La da da la da da la da da. Oh.

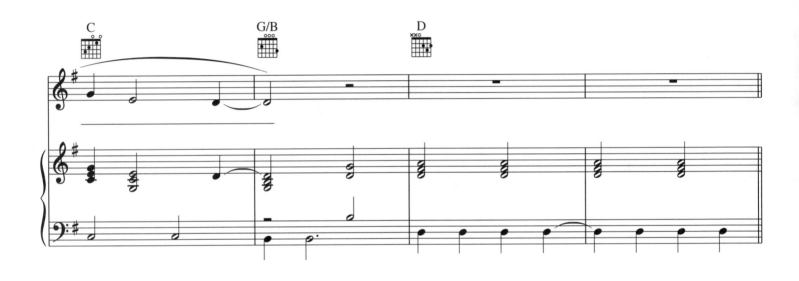

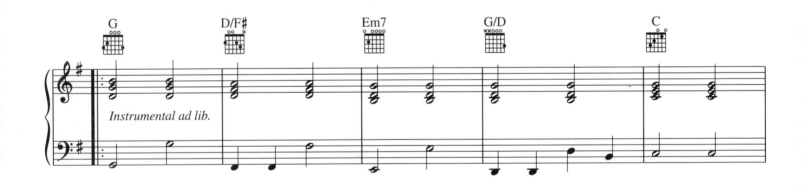

Instrumental ad lib.

Repeat and Fade

Optional Ending

GOODBYE EARL

Words and Music by
DENNIS LINDE

Ma-ry Anne and Wan-da were the best of friends __ all __ through their high school days.__

G C F
Then they tipped their hats and said, "Thank - you, lad - ies. If you hear
C G C
D.S. al Coda
from him, let us know." Well, the
CODA C
die. (Na na na na
F C G F
na na.) Good - bye, Earl. We need a
C N.C. F C G
break. Let's go out to the lake, Earl.

HELLO MR. HEARTACHE

Words and Music by JOHN HADLEY
and MICHAEL HENDERSON

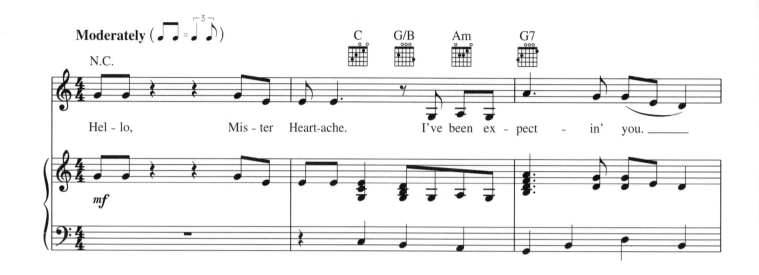

Hel - lo, Mis - ter Heart-ache. I've been ex - pect - in' you. ___

Come in and wear ___ your wel - come out ___ the

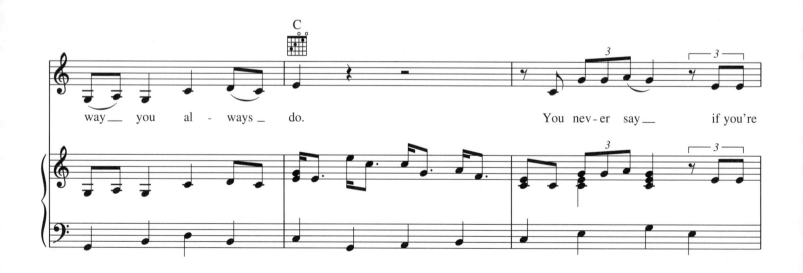

way ___ you al - ways ___ do. You nev - er say ___ if you're

44

Heart-ache. I've been ex - pect - in' you.

DON'T WASTE YOUR HEART

Words and Music by NATALIE MAINES
and EMILY ROBINSON

For the life of __ me __ I can't be-lieve that you're on __ your knees, beg-gin' please. __ All the push - in' a - way __ and put - tin' down, can't you see you're __ get - tin' the run a - round? __ Oh, it's

SIN WAGON

Words and Music by NATALIE MAINES,
EMILY ROBINSON and STEPHONY SMITH

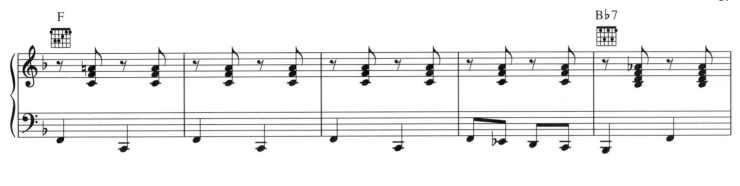

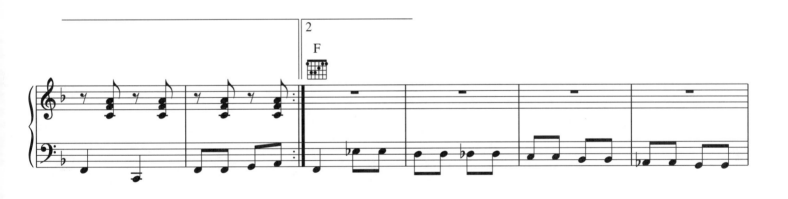

When it's my turn to

sweet sal - va-tion. They may take me with my ____ feet drag-gin', but I'll ____

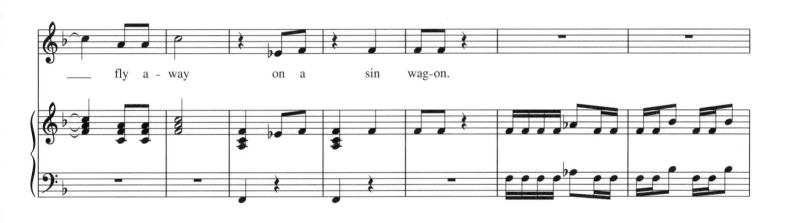

____ fly a - way on a sin wag-on.

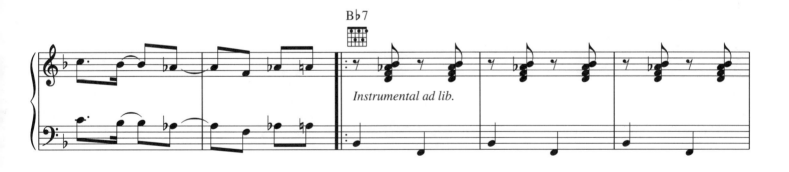

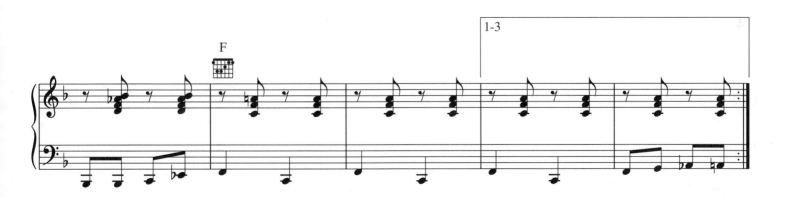

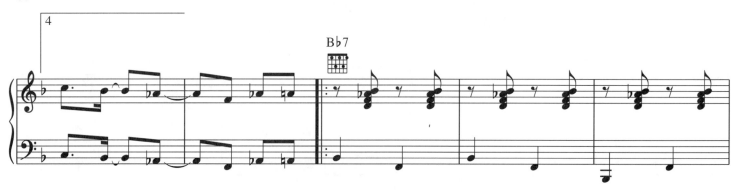

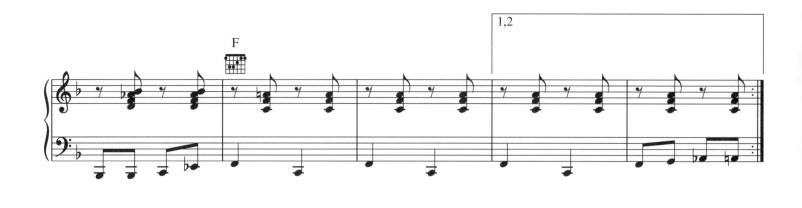

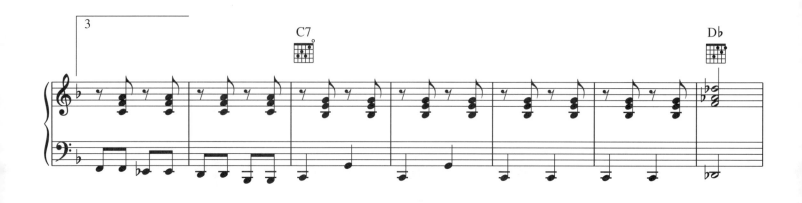

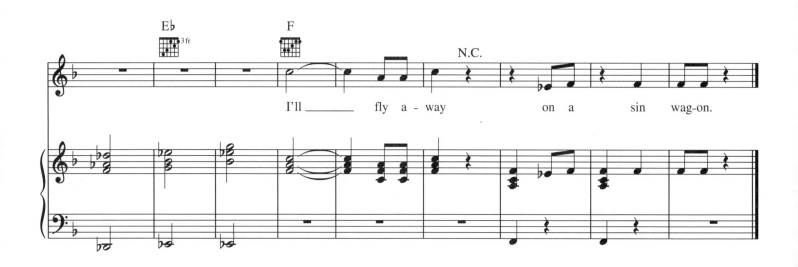

I'll _____ fly a - way on a sin wag-on.

WITHOUT YOU

Words and Music by NATALIE MAINES
and ERIC SILVER

Moderately

I've sure en - joyed ____ the rain, ____ but I'm
Nev - er thought ____ I'd be ____ ly - ing

look - in' for - ward to ____ the sun. ____ You have to feel ____ the pain ____
here with - out ____ you by ____ my side. ____ It seems un - real ____ to me ____

when you lose the love ____ you gave ____ some - one. ____ I
that the life you prom - ised was ____ a lie. ____ You

SOME DAYS YOU GOTTA DANCE

Words and Music by TROY JOHNSON
and MARSHALL MORGAN

Moderately fast

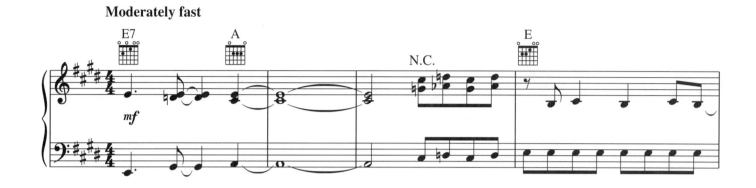

Well, it was a-bout five 'til five __ on Fri - day and we were all __

talk - in' with __ my ba - by o - ver a __

Well I _____ was

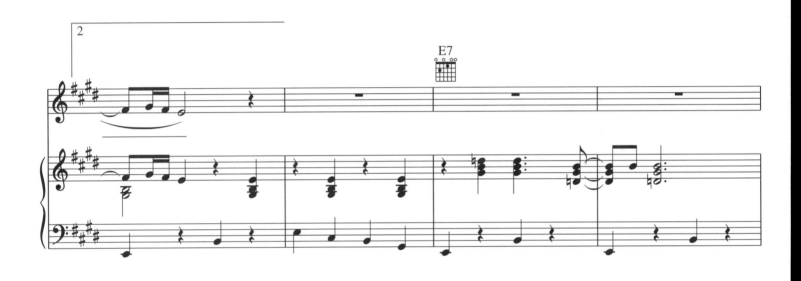

Instrumental ad lib.

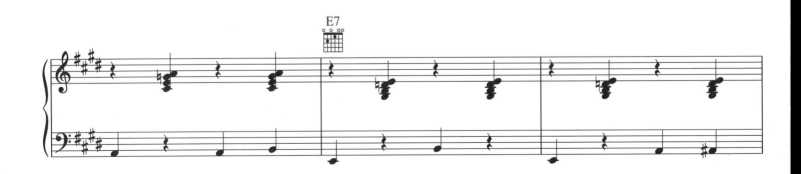

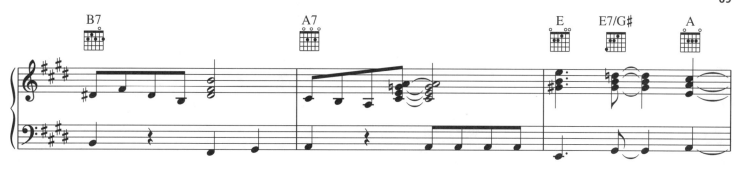

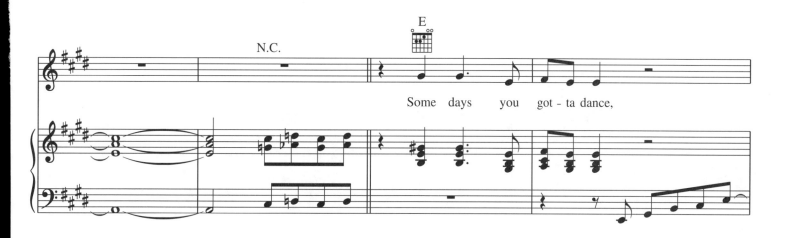

Some days you got-ta dance,

live it up when you get the chance. 'Cause when the world does-n't

make no sense and ___ you're feel-in' just a lit-tle too tense, got-ta

HOLE IN MY HEAD

Words and Music by BUDDY MILLER
and JIM LAUDERDALE

I'm nev - er gon - na win.

Let the games _ be - gin. _____

Yeah, here I go a - gain. _____ I need a

boy like __ you, (I need a boy like __ you, I need a boy like __ you, I need a

HEARTBREAK TOWN

Words and Music by
DARRELL SCOTT

82

LET HIM FLY

Words and Music by
PATTY GRIFFIN